Go, Goats!

KAMA EINHORN

PHOTOGRAPHS BY **JANET HOLMES**

HOUGHTON MIFFLIN HARCOURT
Boston New York

The text type was set in Jolly Good Sans.
Book design by Tom Carling.

Library of Congress Cataloging-in-Publication Data
Names: Einhorn, Kama, 1969- author.
Title: Go, goats! / by Kama Einhorn ; with photos by Janet Holmes.
Description: Boston : Houghton Mifflin Harcourt, [2019] | Series: True tales
of rescue | Audience: Age 7-10. | Audience: Grade 4 to 6.
Identifiers: LCCN 2018052147 | ISBN 9781328767066 (paper over board)
Subjects: LCSH: Goats—Juvenile literature. | Animal sanctuaries—Juvenile
literature. | Animal rescue—Juvenile literature.
Classification: LCC SF383.35 .E36 2019 | DDC 636.3/9--dc23
LC record available at https://lccn.loc.gov/2018052147

Manufactured in Malaysia
TWP 10 9 8 7 6 5 4 3 2 1
4500769247

Author's Note: This book is inspired by the true stories of Catskill Animal Sanctuary, and it's full
of real facts about goats and sanctuary life. But it's also "creative" nonfiction—because goats
don't talk, at least not in ways that humans understand! Some goats mentioned are combinations
of several different ones, and certain details (including locations, events, and timing) have been
changed, and some human dialogue has been reconstructed from memory.

This book is not a manual on animal rescue, nor is it meant to provide any actual directions on caring
for goats or any other animal. Every situation is different. If you see a creature in trouble, contact a
licensed animal rescue group right away.

*For Kathy Stevens
and the many humane humans at
Catskill Animal Sanctuary*

CONTENTS

HOPE & HAVEN:
ANIMAL SANCTUARIES

A sanctuary is a place where living beings are kept safe from harm and free to be themselves.

Humans have created animal sanctuaries—protected places for injured, orphaned, or threatened animals. Some three hundred farm animals—goats, sheep, cows, horses, pigs, donkeys, ducks, geese, chickens, and turkeys—live at Catskill Animal Sanctuary.

Most animal sanctuaries exist because of harm done by humans. Animals at a farm sanctuary are rescued from other farms—usually ones on which animals are used or killed for food—because they are being neglected or mistreated. Some even escape on their own!

The people who run sanctuaries are serious about their work, but they all wish they didn't have to do it in the first place. They wish that animals lived in a better, safer world.

At sanctuaries, humans lend a helping hand.

There's plenty of heartbreak in any sanctuary's story, but there's also lots of happy news. Most sanctuary staff people teach others about the animals, and they share ways to protect them. The more you know about why sanctuaries are important and what people can do to help, the better off all animals—in your neighborhood and all over the planet—will be.

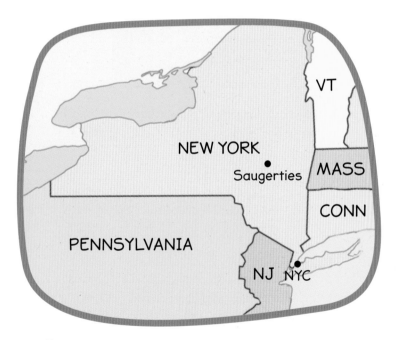

Catskill Animal Sanctuary is in Saugerties, New York.

SANCTUARY STEPS

Each sanctuary is different, but they all do some or all of the following things, in the order below. Catskill Animal Sanctuary handles all four phases:

- **Rescue:** Humans step in, remove animals from harm, and bring them to safety. Rescue situations are usually emergencies.

- **Recovery:** Licensed caregivers treat the animals for injuries or illnesses, create a recovery plan, and let them rest and heal.

- **Rehabilitation:** The caregivers help the animals feel safer and become happier. Sometimes animals learn that from one another.

- **Release:** While some sanctuaries release animals into the wild, a farm sanctuary aims to let many of the animals roam freely.

HEY, KIDS!

I see that Camp Kindness has just begun, and here you are under my favorite weeping willow tree. I remember it from other summers, because goats have very good memories. About thirty of us live here at Catskill Animal Sanctuary, so that's a lot of memories—some good, some bad.

I'm Lucia (pronounced "loo-CHEE-uh"). I'm a member of the Underfoot Family here; we're a group of about fifty goats, sheep, chickens, hens, roosters, geese, and ducks (and one potbellied pig). We roam freely throughout the sanctuary, coming and going from our stalls as we please. We Underfoot goats are like a goat gang! For a long time I was kind of the leader of the goats and sheep, but I've retired to a quieter life.

Allow me to welcome you to my home, campers!

Be warned—goats will nibble any paper you may have in your pockets, although I'm more likely to nuzzle your hands gently with my fuzzy, floppy lips.

You'll start camp every morning under this tree's shade, and then the whole sanctuary will become your classroom. As you spend the day on activities and projects, we animals will be enjoying our recess ... sorry! That's about all we do around here, to tell you the truth.

I live just over there, in the Main Barn. You'll come over later. If you've read *Charlotte's Web*, you can picture what it's like. I suppose I'm a lot like Charlotte, the kind, wise, and gentle old spider. I even have a next-door neighbor like Wilbur the pig.

I sleep in a stall with four sheep: Scully, Junior, Sophie, and cloudy-eyed Hannah, who is nearly blind. Goats get along well with sheep, and the five of us are considered senior citizens. We're roommates because, now that our bodies are aging, we all eat the same kind of soft, special food. I get along with everyone; I'm a pretty easygoing lady. I just had my eighteenth birthday! I have arthritis (my knees get very sore!), a very sensitive belly, and bad teeth—but most days, I feel pretty good.

The humans will be your camp counselors, but I'll also be one of your teachers. You have to sit quietly with me and watch me closely to understand what I have to say, but I promise I will share things that no human can.

Look up. This weeping willow tree we're

under is about seventy feet tall and really thick. As you see, its branches droop low, and the long, silver-green leaves look like feathers. They also look like tears falling down a person's face! When you stand near the trunk, it's as if you're in a secret, safe house with soft, swaying walls. The branches wave in the breeze like curtains, and their shade keeps us cool all summer. If this tree were a person, it would be called "gentle" and "generous." It's so peaceful under here, it's like a mini-sanctuary in the middle of the big sanctuary.

Weeping willows are "gentle giants," just like the cows and horses here. Their roots grow wide, so they need lots of space, just as all the sanctuary residents need lots of land. Good thing the sanctuary is about 150 acres—almost as big as 150 football fields!

Willows are the first trees to grow leaves in spring and the last to lose them in fall, when their leaves have turned golden yellow-green.

There are lots of these trees here, and their leaves are delicious! Any goat tall enough can simply reach up and nibble the leaves. They taste especially great in spring, when we haven't had them all winter. The people here say that the trees never need trimming. "The goats don't let the weeping willows weep!" they say.

The staff also trims branches for a special snack.

Here come Lonnie and Loretta to welcome you, too. They were born here. Baby goats are called kids. Adult males are called bucks or billies, and females are called nannies or does. That would make me a nanny goat— though I suppose by now I'm a *granny* goat!

You'll see how silly we are, but almost every creature here once had a life that was not funny at all. Before most of us arrived, we never had the chance to play. We didn't have healthy food, and we certainly never got any of our favorite gingersnap treats. But as soon as we set one hoof on this land, we sensed that it was different. (I'm one of the luckier ones—I'm here only because my person couldn't keep his land, so he had to find me a new place to live.)

Lonnie and Loretta as kids (baby goats). Kids start life playful, and even as adults, many of us never stop kidding around!

Still, it took some of us a little longer to figure out that humans could be kind. And a few animals here still avoid the humans. But the humans understand. They give us all the space we need to feel safe and secure.

I do hope you'll get the chance to brush some of us. We love it, and so do our visitors! You'll get to do some fun favors for us, too—rub a pig's belly, feed horses, hold a goose, let a calf suck on your fingers, sing to turkeys, and give us goats our willow leaves.

You'll see that humans and nonhuman animals have plenty in common. Just try not to head-butt your friends, as goats tend to do when we play!

You're going to have a great time at camp.

I'm all white ... and sweet as sugar.

PART 1

RESCUE

Helping Hands

CHAPTER 1

Taking it in

Our eyes let us see the world differently from the way humans see it. Look at Cupid's eyes. See how our pupils are rectangular, not round like yours? That's so we can have peripheral vision, which humans might call seeing more widely.

Like Cupid's, my eyes are golden, unlike those of any human. But don't worry about the differences in our eyes. Like goats, the humans here have seen the same sad sights—animals being treated badly. One day, a few Octobers ago, they couldn't believe their eyes.

It was after breakfast on an ordinary day, and my arthritis was really bothering me. My

Our pupils let us keep an eye out for trouble as we're eating from the ground.

joints are in bad shape; you can hear them clicking when I walk! I had tasted turmeric (a mustard-orange spice) and ground black pepper in my extra food pellets. Eating those spices helps me walk more easily, making me not so stiff and rigid in my hind end. The humans try spices before they give me the more serious drugs.

In the kitchen area next to our stall, the staff and volunteers were chopping up big crimson pomegranates and bright orange mandarins—special treats for the ducks and geese. (What about the turkeys, you ask? Don't worry about them; they would be eating especially well very soon, because the staff had just invited a bunch of humans to a Thanksgiving party called "How to Serve a Turkey," where the turkeys are served their very own vegetarian dinner! The humans who work here don't eat meat, dairy, or eggs. To them, animals aren't food.)

On the floor of the kitchen, a volunteer squatted and used two fingers to rub JR the rooster's wattle in gentle circles. As JR relaxed his feathery body against her jeans, his lentil-size orange eyes closed slightly. It was such a peaceful morning!

But all of a sudden, things changed. The humans started rushing around. The crackling and blaring of their walkie-talkies startled poor, shy Hannah the sheep. They moved fast, and then they all disappeared. Later, I heard about why they'd left.

They drove an hour north, where they met a few police officers who were waiting for them at the edge of an overgrown field. On that field stood a small, shabby barn made of rotting wood. Together they went inside, their round pupils widening in the dark. As their eyes adjusted, they took in a scene they wished they'd be able to forget (and still haven't).

Two hundred sick goats, cows, and pigs were crammed into the filthy barn. All were starving, weak, and terrified. Twenty more were dead. And there was a lot of poop on the cement floor.

A person known as a "backyard butcher" was responsible for this mess. He had been raising the animals behind his home, selling the female cows' and goats' milk, and slaughtering the cows and pigs so he could sell their meat. Obviously, he hadn't been caring for them.

It was a house of horrors. "The smell alone will give me nightmares," I heard a human say late that night.

The police had found out about this place three weeks earlier, when a sheep escaped and was hit by a car. The police returned the sheep to the farm and went to check on her the next day. They saw the barn only from the outside, but they didn't like what little they saw. They called the Hudson Valley Society for the Prevention of Cruelty to Animals (SPCA) to help investigate, and the SPCA had to work fast to find a safe home for the animals.

Because the man had not been providing food, water, or medical care, the police arrested him for animal neglect.

The SPCA called our sanctuary and three others in New York State, and staff from all four sanctuaries rushed to help. It was the largest-ever animal rescue in the area!

Four truckloads of animals were taken straight to Cornell University's College of Veterinary Medicine's Hospital for Animals in Ithaca, New York. And the humans here at Catskill Animal Sanctuary said they would make room for twenty-seven of the goats—nine males, eighteen females. All the animals were led (or carried) out of that barn into metal trailers attached to trucks, and the journey began.

When they arrived here, some goats were carried from the trailers; some stumbled out on their own. The goats weren't used to light, and their pupils got small. Some seemed calm and relieved, others stayed skittish and terrified. They were all covered in sores, and many had clumps of hair missing.

There are no trolls guarding the bridges here— just Nellie and Caroline!

None of them had ever known anyplace other than that tiny barn, and they had no way of knowing that good things were coming soon. Many of them must have thought that all humans were even meaner than that troll from the "Three Billy Goats Gruff" story, the one who wouldn't let the three little goats cross his bridge.

The backyard butcher was the only human they'd ever known, so to them all humans were trolls. I don't like to speak badly of humans, as all the humans I've known have been very good to me. But dare I say that any human who treats animals that way is certainly behaving as a troll would!

29

CHAPTER 2

A HURTING HERD

You didn't have to be a vet to see that this rescued herd was a mess. Right away, all twenty-seven goats were brought into a large empty barn that had lots of clean straw on the ground. The vets and the staff would certainly have plenty of work to do in the days and weeks to come.

Every single goat had lice and mites, plus fungal skin infections. Most had breathing problems. When the vets listened to their lungs with stethoscopes, they heard rattling and wheezing. Some had pneumonia. Many had the orf virus, an infection that covers our mouths in scabby sores. Their eyes were all drippy and infected. Their hooves were in such bad shape, they could barely stand or walk. Many of them had fever or diarrhea. Nearly all of them needed antibiotics.

Stressed and depressed as they were, many refused to eat.

CAS
Catskill Animal Sanctuary

Name _Goat herd_   Animal Record
Arrival Date _10/10/15_
Species _goats_   Birthdate _unknown_
Age _unknown_ Sex _9 males 18 females_ Breed _mixed breeds_
Description/ID/ Markings_____

History/Rescue Story _rescued along w/other animals (sent to FS, WFAS, Skylands) from Hamptonburgh NY (orange co.) hoarder & backyard butcher_

Conditions/Issues _intestinal parasites ORF, lice, respiratory issues some females may be pregnant (could be complications)_

Outgoing Information Adopted_____ Deceased_____
Adopter Information_____ Date____
_____
_____
Sponsors_____
_____
_____

The humans keep files on each rescue.

When it comes to water, goats are like camels. We can store a lot in our bodies for when we need it. Because the herd hadn't been given any water for such a long time, they were dehydrated, so the humans put out big bowls of warm water.

Most of the goats were shivering, and many were so thin, they needed goat coats.

31

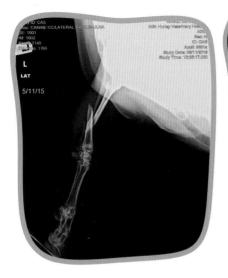

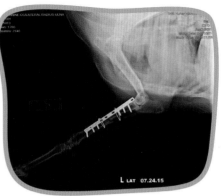

Vets can see inside us!

Usually, only sick, old, or baby goats need them (I wear my cozy new red coat almost all winter long now).

Though the humans were feeling overwhelmed by the huge task of helping this herd, they had fun naming the goats. There was Bea, Carla, Chelsea, Cora, Corduroy, Darla, Dickon, Dobby, Dolly, Don Quixote, Dulce, Edith, Jacquelyn, Leah, Louise, Lydia, Mia, Priscilla, Sancho, Sandy,

Sven, Vanna, Vincent, Waddles, and ZZ.

The humans looked like astronauts in their special white suits, which protected them from the lice that could jump off the goats and onto people. Besides making us uncomfortable, parasites such as lice can drink our blood and cause anemia, a blood problem that makes us really weak.

Staff listened to each goat's lungs.
They usually didn't like what they heard.

33

The staff knew how expensive it would be to help this herd. They'd need to raise a lot of money to renovate the old barn, build a new barn, pay for lots of vet visits, buy a ton of straw, and neuter the males.

The sanctuary asked for online donations of $27 (since there were twenty-seven goats in the rescue), but many people gave more. Soon, many generous people had donated the money the sanctuary needed. But there was plenty more work to do, because the blood tests came back with some big news.

Four of the females—Edith, Jacquelyn, Vanna, and Leah—were pregnant! No one had known that, because they were so thin. The vet said that they all seemed like first-time moms, but because of their health conditions, he couldn't guarantee that the babies would be born alive.

Lucia's Math Class

Okay, I know camp isn't school, but you should learn this because you never know when you may have to weigh a scared, hard-to-move goat. There's a flat scale here, like a tabletop, sitting right on the floor, but to weigh the average adult goat, all you need is a cloth measuring tape and a calculator.

How much does Rhue weigh? Humans estimate our weight by using a little math.

1. Look at Rhue's measurements.

2. Multiply: heart girth x heart girth x distance between shoulder and hip =

3. Divide by 300 to find out Rhue's approximate weight.

ANSWER: Almost 131 pounds. HOW YOU GET THIS ANSWER: When you multiply 33, 33, and 36 you get 39,204. Divide that by 300 and you get 130.68.

*Girth is the measurement around the middle of something, like a person's waist.

And big news kept coming. About half the herd's bloodwork had tested positive for a bacterium called CL (Caseous lymphadenitis, "KAY-zee-us lim-fuh-duh-NIGHT-us"), which can cause swollen sores on the insides and outsides of goats' bodies. It

PASTURE PEDICURES

The rescued herd was limping because their hooves were overgrown and rotted away. So the vets and staff did serious pedicures on every goat! That's more than one hundred hooves!

Our hooves are made of keratin, like your fingernails. If we're kept in a barn and can't climb on rocks, our hooves grow out of control. It's as if your fingernails grew and grew—then you wouldn't be able to use your hands to do anything. It's also very painful. If our hooves twist, our legs get all hobbled and can become permanently deformed. Our gait, or way of walking, is all messed up. A well-trimmed hoof is flat on the bottom.

turned out they'd be okay, and most of them would never even get sick from CL, but it is contagious. Those goats would need to be quarantined (kept separately) in a new barn and a big fenced-in field called the Q Field (Q for quarantine).

To treat this condition, the humans use a hoof pick to remove rocks, gravel, mud, and manure that get ground into our hooves. They spray them with soapy water and dry them.

Next, they use hoof trimmers, which are like giant nail clippers or scissors.

Last, they file them flat with a giant file called a rasp.

Presto—a goat with happy, healthy hooves!

37

CHAPTER 3

FOUR MOMS, EIGHT KIDS

The four pregnant females were weak and malnourished; they'd been starving. They were also barely adults themselves. The humans knew that the chances of the babies being born prematurely—too early and too small—were high. The risk of preemies meant that there would probably be some middle-of-the-night emergency calls to the vets.

The humans quickly turned a quiet end of the barn into a maternity ward. To protect the moms-to-be from drafts, the walls were higher than those of the other stalls. Heat lamps hung from the roof, and extra straw bedding covered the ground.

As the rest of the herd slowly grew healthier, the lovely autumn turned into frosty winter. The staff started watching the moms for signs that the kids were about to be born. One sign that a goat is going into labor is that her udders form a waxy substance on them. A mom might paw at the ground or keep lying down and getting up, as if she just can't get comfortable. She might pant, breathe fast and heavy, stop eating, or rearrange her straw bedding, creating a little nest.

Finally, on New Year's Day, Edith's waxy udder was the clue that her kid was coming soon.

Within a few hours, the humans saw a round, dark bulge that looked like a clear bag of water coming out of Edith, who lay flat on the straw. As it burst, a tiny nose poked out! But the kid stayed where it was, and Edith did not move. The humans stood back and let mom do her hard work. Edith gave a push, and then the humans saw the kid's shoulders, and out slipped a tiny white kid with biscuit-colored spots. It was soaking wet, and its eyes were wide-open. It looked like a little alien, its head a strange shape, rounder than most. But there it was, alive. It was a girl!

Just as doctors do with human babies, the vet clamped the umbilical cord two inches from the kid's belly and snipped it with clean, sharp scissors. He cleaned carefully around the kid's bellybutton so it wouldn't get infected. "Happy birthday, little one!" he called out happily. The staff named her Lillian.

Lillian, flopping weakly in the hay in a puddle of slime and blood, was the first truly lucky member of this herd. Raising her wobbly head and shoulders, she started shaking off her

wetness like a dog after a bath. It was her birthday, and it was also the first day of 2016.

It was the first page in a new chapter for the whole herd.

Edith seemed a little confused at first. She looked at her damp new kid with an expression that said, *Who are you, and what just happened?* The humans offered Edith warm water with a little molasses to replace her lost energy. At the same time, other members of the team wrapped Lillian in a towel and suctioned out her nose, just as they would a human baby, so she could breathe well. She started bleating loudly right away!

They weighed her on a tiny scale, the kind pediatricians use. She didn't weigh nearly enough, and she would need an igloo—a tiny plastic dome that provides extra warmth for kids who need it. They took her temperature and then, as fast as they could, left mom and kid alone. Edith was tired, but she put her hoof over Lillian. Then she went to work licking her clean, then nursing her a little. In about twenty minutes Lillian was already standing up!

The tiny kid looked as if she were standing on tippy-toes. She swayed from side to side, staggering and wobbling and weaving, toppling over and getting right back up. The whole time, Lillian seemed to be moving sideways.

After her little standing adventure, Lillian lay back down on the hay and fell asleep. But Edith, already a worried mom, pawed at her to wake her up and nurse some more.

The humans also acted like adoring aunts and uncles—
they even made Lillian a coat!

Whenever Lillian cried, Edith looked at her
closely to figure out what she needed.

Lillian was ridiculously adorable, and for a few weeks she was the center of attention.

But a few weeks later, on January 24, Lillian was no longer the center of attention, as Jacquelyn went into labor. The maternity ward was totally prepared. There were small dog crates that had blankets inside, and more blankets ready to cover the crates as the kids slept in them to stay warm. Boxes of milk bottles and powdered formula were everywhere.

Jacquelyn's labor started out the same as Edith's. A kid slipped out, and the humans announced, "It's another girl!" They named her Lonnie.

But soon things changed. Fifteen minutes later, another kid followed. "It's a girl again!"

the humans cried. The kid, who they named Loretta, lay quietly on the slimy straw.

And then ... fifteen minutes after that ... another kid! (Turns out that many goats are born as twins or triplets.) "How about that! It's a girl!" the humans cried. They named her Lulu—another L name, for the "Love Sisters."

Lulu was teeny-tiny and not breathing well. The vet used a special tube to blow oxygen close to her nose, but it didn't help. Lonnie and Loretta were a good size, heavier than Lillian had been, but Lulu just wasn't big enough, and she lived only a few more hours.

That was hard for the humans to see, though Jacquelyn seemed preoccupied caring for her two healthy kids. Lonnie and Loretta were small but sturdy, and after two days they were playing with each other. They needed vitamin B shots and extra bottles, but they were on the right track.

The herd now had three new members, and these kids would get to nurse as long as they liked. As long as they all stayed healthy, they could live with their moms throughout their lives. They were lucky, as it's rare for most goats in the United States to stay with their moms for even one day. Farmers raise female goats for their milk, which they sell. That milk is often made into cheese. It may seem natural for a goat to be milked, but when a goat is being raised only for her milk, it's not that simple.

Let me explain. Just like humans and cows, female goats make milk only after they have babies. Most farmers want their goats to make milk all the time so it can be sold. So the farmers keep the goats pregnant as much of the time as they can. When the goats give birth, their kids are taken away immediately so that their moms' milk can be sold rather than used to feed the kids.

Male kids are killed right away because they can't make any milk for the farmers to sell. Female kids start getting used to making milk as soon as they're old enough.

Other goats are raised for their meat, not their milk. They're killed at about four months old, even though we can live for eighteen years. About a million and a half goats are slaughtered each year in the United States.

Obviously, the humans here don't raise us for milk or meat. They tried to give the new moms and their kids enough space, even though they checked on them a lot. Some nights were so cold that the kids were brought to the infirmary stalls close to the Main Barn, where there was a regular heater, the kind humans use.

As tired as the humans were, they were prepared for two more moms to give birth. Good thing, because just a few hours after Jacquelyn's triplets were born, Vanna was ready to add to the herd.

"We've got another girl!" a human cried. And there on the straw lay little Annie.

Soon enough . . . there was Tula. "Hey, big surprise! It's a girl!"

And then . . . there lay Violet, the size of a potato. "Oh hello, girl! Welcome to the world!"

Scientists studied mama goats and kids one year after they were separated. The moms notice their kids' bleats more than those of other kids—our families are as important to us as yours is to you!

Violet was different from any of the others. She weighed only one pound. The humans just looked at her, amazed, hoping she'd stay alive. These three kids needed vitamin B shots and extra bottles, too.

And a few hours after that, Leah, the fourth pregnant goat, gave birth to . . . yup, a girl! The humans named her Libby. After having just witnessed two sets of triplet births, they watched carefully to see if another kid was on its way behind her, but they knew that if after 30 minutes a mom seems comfortable, she's done.

The humans said Leah was the "most maternal" mom of the four—the most loving and attentive. Leah never took her eyes off Libby, and Libby was the most active of all seven! But like most baby goats, Libby spent most of her of time nuzzling her mama.

The air remained frosty. As January turned

into February, the humans continued to feed
the kids extra bottles around the clock. The
herd had grown stronger and happier, and
now they had seven new little-girl members.
Their new life had begun.

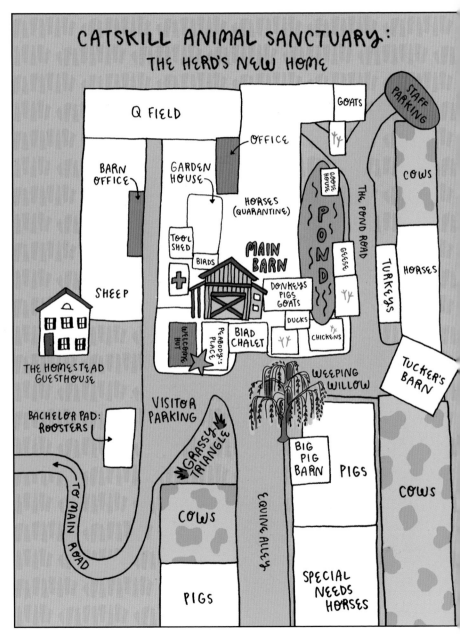

PART 2

RECOVERY

Creature Care

CHAPTER 4

A HaPPiER HeRD

Resting and recovering was easier for some members of the herd than for others. The potato-size preemie, Violet, had the hardest time of all. For one thing, she hadn't developed normally when she was growing inside Vanna. Her legs were deformed; she didn't stand or walk the way she should. She was so little that she couldn't keep herself warm, so she wore tiny sweaters all the time.

Another bigger problem was that from the moment she was born, Vanna pushed Violet away and wouldn't let her nurse. This happens sometimes with animals. No one knows for sure why. It could have been that because Violet was so small, Vanna didn't think she would survive. Vanna didn't have

much milk; maybe her instinct told her to give it all to the other two kids. Or maybe she thought Violet had a disease that would harm the other babies. The humans would never know, but they did know that Violet would depend on them for survival.

Violet spent the first night of her life in a cat carrier at the home of two staff members, Kellie and Matt. Kellie fed her warm formula in a kitten bottle every two hours, with Violet standing up as if she were nursing from her mom.

Kellie and Matt loved having Violet in their home, even though Violet peed everywhere. Kellie tried to use an extra-small puppy diaper, but Violet was too small even for that, and it fell off!

After one month, all seven kids, including Violet, weighed enough to safely move them,

Little Violet
at three
months old.

with their moms, to stalls near me in the
Main Barn (or to the Q Field). Right away
I became a granny goat. I liked comforting
the kids when their moms weren't around. I

looked out for them and tried to show them good manners (which I suppose was kind of pointless). I had plenty of love and affection to spare, and I felt like their guardian.

Violet did just fine in the Main Barn. Shy Jacquelyn "adopted" her, and she still lives in a stall with Jacquelyn and her kids, Lonnie and Loretta.

Violet's a real loner, more than most goats, and she's just kind of . . . different somehow. Her brain may not have developed normally. She's also a major

Lonnie and Violet.

head-butter. But none of that seems to matter to the humans—they're just crazy about her. And she's every bit as happy as the rest of us.

Kids are wild about Violet, too.

I spent lots of time with the kids, letting them know that life here at the sanctuary is good. In our own goat language, I told them that soon winter would end and the frozen ground would thaw. The days would get longer, and we could wander around even later each evening. Barn swallows and bluebirds would flutter around the Main Barn, tweeting the good news that spring was finally coming to the Catskills. There would be fresh rain showers and less of the mud we hate.

I told them that after spring, there would be warm summer breezes and delicious willow branches cut just for us. In autumn, there would be mushy pumpkin chunks and crisp apple slices for afternoon snack. The sanctuary goodness would go on and on! I told them I'd be right there to show them everything. And their moms really appreciated my babysitting.

The goats who went to the Q Field also settled in well. The Q Field is huge and has a good barn and playground, which some humans had built. The land slopes slightly, so the goats have a dry place to stand (we hate standing where it's wet; water rots our hooves away). It has lots of rocks to climb on, and the bright early-morning sun that floods the barn feels great.

The only thing the "Q goats" don't love about this goat paradise is the fence, which was designed with our natural cleverness in mind. Unfortunately, goats don't get a vote! The Q goats stand on their hind legs, front hooves resting on the fence tops, and peer out, trying to crush the fencing to step over it. That's why the gates open inward.

We can also use our strong horns to butt through fences (as I remember fondly from

my younger days). Humans have to check and fix the fences often because we're super active and we love to explore. Goats can be expert escape artists.

As the herd settled into the Main Barn and the Q Field, spring returned to the Catskills. As always, the willow trees were the first to grow their delicious leaves, and some of us could reach up for them. I don't reach anymore, but some goats—maybe for the good of their herd, no one knows for sure— will pull the branches lower and actually share with other goats once they've gotten their own fill. The humans brought some around to the rest of us. Our world was getting greener and greener.

Our winter bedding was raked out, and we got fresh straw. The air and everything around us smelled new. Outside our barn,

Dolores's overhead banquet.

the world was waking up. It was my sixteenth spring.

CHAPTER 5

BROWSING & BELLIES

Hey, kids, it's time for your lunch break. I wish I could join you at the Homestead for the delicious lunch you'll make together. Food is a very big deal around here for all of us.

First thing every morning, the humans bring me a small metal bowl with a quarter of a cup of "senior grain" pellets. Twice a day, I'm given piles of dry hay, plus well-chopped hay in a big black plastic bowl. It's chopped because our gums pull away from our teeth as we age (like people's do), so some of our teeth get loose or poke out, making it harder to chew. I have a little underbite, and I've learned to chew slowly and carefully.

It's best for our digestion if we really grind our food.

I love my dry hay, which is put in a mound right on the floor of my stall. Like I always have, I nuzzle it with my nose as I eat. I bury my face in the pile, grabbing the tangle with my lips and using them to pull up clumps. The hay kind of hangs from my mouth to the ground, making me look like a human really enjoying a bowl of spaghetti. Then I'll start to chew in my special goat way. Our upper jaws are wider than our lower jaws, so we use only one side of our mouths to grind the food—and we chew in a rotating motion that looks like a figure eight.

For much of the herd, putting on weight was the most important part of recovery. The humans know exactly what we need. We're herbivores, which means we eat only plants. Morning and afternoon, the food tractor rolls around. As soon as we hear it, most of us follow it happily, rushing and bumping into one another. I've stopped running after it, though. We old folks wait calmly; we know it's coming. I don't hurry anywhere, not anymore—I just saunter over to the barn in my own sweet time.

Aside from the sound of the truck, we also hear the humans preparing food in the kitchen. Noises from the kitchen are always great news. We hear lids slapping, grain plinking into plastic and metal buckets, knives clicking on the big metal table, and pellets being poured out of bins, bags, or boxes. Boy, do those sounds get our attention! If we're in our stalls with the doors closed, many of us angle our bodies toward the kitchen, standing up and waiting, our hooves up against the stall walls. (The younger ones will do this while jumping up and down on their hind legs! They peer down the aisle as if to say, *Is mine coming yet?*)

Like Arthur and Stencil, most goats will nibble on anything—cardboard, paper, clothes—to find out what's edible. Leah even nibbles on zippers.

When all's quiet in the Main Barn, you can hear us munching our dry hay, making a gentle rustling sound. You can hear Buddy the blind horse grinding and crunching his food, and my pig neighbor's jowls flapping. It's usually quite dark in the barn, though light slants in during the afternoon. The air in those sunbeams looks dusty. For older animals like me, feeding time is quiet and peaceful, and we nap afterward. Thelma even uses her nose to make a little nest of her leftover hay, and she naps right there.

Sometimes the hay is served in the aisle of the barn, placed in containers that look like a cross between cages and big metal bike racks. Everyone tries to find a good spot from which to pull the hay out; some eat from the top and some kneel down low.

There's a giant whiteboard in the kitchen that has information for staff and volunteers as they prepare our food, plus directions about all our special diets (there's even a note saying that some of us are allowed only half a gingersnap as a treat ... a real shame).

Gingersnap time!

The Browser Café

Goats are browsers. We nibble a little here, a little there—mostly weeds, bushes, leaves, tree bark, twigs, vines, and shrubs. Deer are browsers, too (goats are like first cousins to deer). Sheep, on the other hand, are grazers, eating mostly grass. (There's an old Greek saying: "Goats look up, sheep look down.") Here's the menu the humans made:

HAY

The hay at the Browser Café is never moldy or dusty. It's a high-quality gourmet blend of long-stemmed dried grass that is cut later in the season (making it the most nutritious):

✔ timothy grass

✔ barley

✔ orchard grass

✔ alfalfa

WARNING: Not too much alfalfa, or goats will get sick! Mostly for older goats and those who need to gain weight.

Hay comes in packed chunks called bales. Bales are separated into six-inch-thick slices called "flakes," and I get one flake every day.

FIELD SPECIALS (SUMMER & SPRING ONLY)

✔ dandelion weeds

✔ thistle

✔ roses off the rosebush *oh, well!*

✔ blackberries

✔ brambles

SENIOR SPECIALS

Some old guys and girls with bad (or fewer) teeth get moistened grain pellets, which are easier to chew and digest than hay.

Clean, fresh drinking water is available at all times.

SERVING SUGGESTIONS

✔ Less crowding equals less fighting! In smaller stalls, arrange the hay in a doughnut shape so that some goats can stand "inside the doughnut" while they eat and others can stand around the outside.

✔ Remember, an older or timid goat might get bullied and pushed away from the food, so create multiple feeding areas. You may have to feed some goats separately to make sure they get enough to eat.

DESSERT

Goats love variety and surprises. Some favorites:

A Fall Favorite!

✔ gingersnaps

✔ willow branches

✔ apple slices

✔ summer strawberries

✔ pumpkin chunks, mushy part included

✔ carrots, apples, bananas, watermelon, peanuts, graham crackers, saltines, bread, horse treats, and fruit and veggie scraps.

KIDS' MENU

Kids' stomachs aren't developed enough to have hay until they're about eight weeks old. Until then, they get:

✔ mom's milk or formula

✔ comfrey leaves

✔ sunflower seeds

✔ vegetable trimmings

✳ A SPECIAL NOTE ON STRAW

Goats might eat it, but straw is meant to be bedding, not food!

Hermione browsing.

Let me escort you up the hill toward the Homestead, where you'll cook and eat lunch every day this week. I'm sure you'll enjoy the meal you make there. It's pretty hot and humid today, isn't it? Maybe later you'll get to run through the sprinklers. We love to play, too (just not with water).

As we stroll, let me tell you about our stomachs. I hear that you guys each have only one

stomach. A drumroll, please . . . goats have four, yes, four stomachs.

Like cows, we're ruminants. That means we have four different stomach compartments, or chambers, in which we digest our food. As ruminants, we "chew our cud." I'll start at the beginning.

The sun gives off crazy amounts of energy, and it's stored in plants. We get almost all of our energy by eating plants. We can do this because our stomachs let us get everything we need from plants. I'll show you.

We take a bite of grass, and as we chew, the grass mixes with our saliva. When we swallow, the grass goes down the esophagus to our first stomach chamber-the rumen.

FOUR STOMACHS

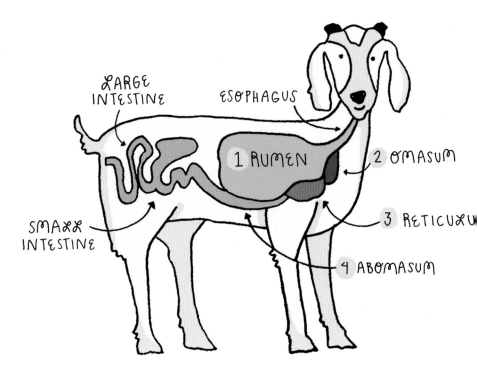

LARGE INTESTINE

ESOPHAGUS

1 RUMEN

2 OMASUM

3 RETICULU

SMALL INTESTINE

4 ABOMASUM

1 The rumen is huge, and it's why our bodies look so wide around the middle. It's like a big factory for breaking down food.

It's really important that all the fiber we eat gets broken down completely. So every once in a while, the rumen shoots a wad of food—called the cud—right back up to our mouths to be rechewed! That's called "chewing our cud," and as we rechew, we burp a lot to get rid of gas. Then we swallow it again for a second round of digestion. The rumen works so hard, it makes its own heat and keeps us warm.

2 Next stop is the omasum. Its lining looks all "foldy," like a cabbage leaf. All that surface area allows it to absorb all the water in the food particles.

3 Then the food goes to the reticulum, which looks like a honeycomb. It's like a filter—anything we eat that can't be digested stays there.

4 Last stop is the abomasum, which is most similar to your human stomach. Acid and enzymes turn food into protein and the food moves into our intestines, which are a lot like yours.

Like Sam, we may look for treats in our friends' coats!

Sometimes you can hear and see our rumens working, once every minute, through our skin on our left side! I think they sound pretty, like the ocean, or like wind through the trees. Humans can also hear them with a stethoscope.

All this talk of stomachs makes me want to go back to my stall to snack on some of the hay I saved from breakfast.

I think I'll also visit the salt block. In addition to the fiber we get from hay, we need certain minerals. The salt block looks like a brick the size of a shoebox, and it's made of salt, plus some limestone, vitamin A, vitamin D, and vitamin E. Humans designed it for us.

Even though we get plenty of food, lots of us follow the feed trucks and gobble hay as it's brought around the whole sanctuary . We'll even hop on!

Our need for salt motivates us to lick it. And salt keeps us thirsty, so we drink more water, which helps us digest our hay. Very clever, these humans.

Poppy thinks the salt lick is all hers.

CHAPTER 6

BODiES & BREEDS

All that food, water, vet care, and love boils down to achieving one goal—a healthy, happy goat.

There are two types of goats: domestic goats (usually raised and bred for meat and milk) and wild mountain goats, who live in rocky parts of the Northwest United States. All goats are related to antelopes, sheep, and cattle. We at the Sanctuary are domestic.

Mountain goat

Just like dogs, there are many breeds of goats—such as LaManchas, with their elfin ears; Nubians, with long, floppy ears; and Kashmirs, with long, silky wool. I'm a mix, and so is Violet.

Our horn's rings show how old we are, just like the rings on tree trunks.

Many humans think that male goats smell bad, but female goats would disagree.

We don't have any upper front teeth. We use our bottom teeth and our strong tongues.

Our upper lips are prehensile—like monkey tails and human fingers, they can wrap and grab. When we nibble treats from your hands, you'll feel soft tickles.

Some of us have long, silky tufts of hair on our chins.

Our hooves are cloven—we have two separate hard toes that we spread apart for balance. We look as if we're standing on tiptoes!

80

Our soft hair is often shiny. If we're sick, it might be rough or dull.

Our stout bodies give us a strong center of balance, so we can stand confidently on steep land or rocks.

Our "withers" is the area between our shoulder blades. Humans pinch us here to find out if we have enough fat.

Our legs can "lock" in a way that humans find stubborn (it's hard for them to move us). They can "scoot" us by walking next to us and pushing.

Most of us have knobby, callused knees; the hair is all worn off (we kneel a lot, and use our knees for balance as we lie down and get up).

Goats and sheep hang out together, but we're different—and sometimes humans can't tell us apart. Hannah and I will explain!

GOAT   OR

Tails usually stick up.

Hair doesn't need shearing or combing.

Horns (if we have them) grow in a V shape.

Can be more independent.

More confident around people at first.

Usually rebellious, playful explorers.

Browers (eat leaves, twigs, vines, and shrubs). Goats look up!

Hard to keep within a fence.

In a fight, goats will rear up on their hind legs and come down hard to butt heads.

May have beards.

May like to be sung to.

SHEEP?

Tails hang down.

Most sheep grow woolly coats that are sheared at least once a year.

Wider-set horns curl around in loops.

Can become upset if separated from their flock.

Often timid around people at first.

Usually serene, mellow.

Grazers (eat grass from ground). Sheep look down!

Easy to keep within a fence!

Sheep will back up and charge forward to butt heads.

Do not have beards.

Most sheep LOVE being sung to.

But goats and sheep have at least one thing in common—neither of us like to get our hooves wet!

Many goats, one sheep. That's me in the background.

PART 3

REHABILITATION

Healing the Herd

CHAPTER 7

BARN LIFE

At six in the morning, just before the humans arrive, the Main Barn is our own private world.

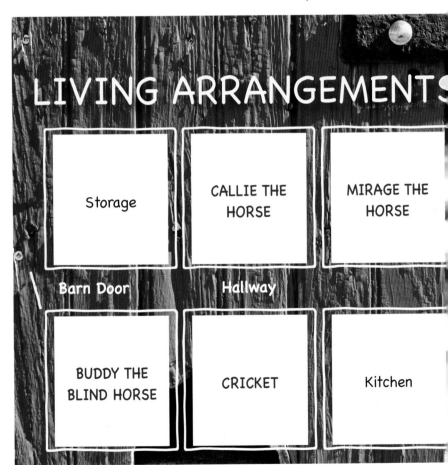

LIVING ARRANGEMENTS

Storage	CALLIE THE HORSE	MIRAGE THE HORSE

Barn Door   Hallway

BUDDY THE BLIND HORSE	CRICKET	Kitchen

All you hear are roosters cock-a-doodle-dooing, ducks quacking, horses whinnying, and sparrows and cardinals singing. Though many of us roam free all day, we rest quietly in our stalls at night.

IN THE MAIN BARN

SISTER MARY FRANCES THE POTBELLIED PIG	THE SMALL GOATS: JACQUELYN, LONNIE, VIOLET, BEA	BEST FRIENDS: OLLIE, TIGGER, HERMOINE
	Hallway	Barn Door
THE SENIORS: LUCIA, SCULLY, JUNIOR, SOPHIE, HANNAH	THE LAMB FAMILY: BERTHA, LENA, LAVERNE, LIZA, SUZI, SENECA, DAVEY, STEWART	THE OLD MARRIED COUPLE: THELMA & CERBERUS (GOATS)

The Main Barn is where life starts to feel normal for most of us.

The Main Barn contains a long row of rooms (our stalls) along an aisle, like a hallway. (Some chickens seem to think the aisle's a fashion runway as they strut through a few times a day, clucking and pecking at the ground.) And it gets noisy: *bleat, chirp, baa, neigh, whinny, oink!* (And of course, the fast *eh-eh-eh-eh* of us goats. Those sounds can mean different things at different times. They could mean, *Oh, I am so happy and alive!* or *This is my safe place!* or *That was my spot!* or *You're my best friend!* or *Get away from my treats!*)

The newest herd had already survived the worst—they'd been rescued. Most of them had recovered physically. But many stayed fearful of humans, and some were angry, too. So it was time for rehabilitation, which is about not only surviving, but thriving.

Rehabilitation is about healing our spirits. Once we've gotten the medical attention we need, "rehab" can really start. The humans pay close attention to our mood, our likes, our dislikes, and our quirks, getting to know each of us as the individuals that we are. It takes lots of patience and love, and the humans have plenty of both. It's a good thing, 'cause most of us sure do need lots of that after what we've been through.

Rehab means something different to each animal. It's the humans' job to figure this out for each of us. We each heal at our own pace, on our own terms. If we need space, we get it. The humans decide what diet and medical treatments will keep us happiest

and healthiest. They also figure out who should be kept together in stalls and who should be separated (we do a "stall shuffle" as the humans move us around for different reasons).

For a few months, Hannah and I lived together in a smaller stall in the Main Barn. Then we moved to a bigger one so that three senior sheep—Scully, Sophie, and Junior—could join us. All the sheep are pretty shy, and we're great stall-mates. We're across from the kitchen now because it's at the middle of the barn, where it's warmest!

Unlike that horrific barn where the herd had been so mistreated, this barn was designed with only our comfort and well-being in mind. We have plenty of space, and it's well ventilated to keep moisture from building up and getting us cold. We really struggle when

G🜚AT GOSSiP

Now that you know the basics of who's who, wanna know what else?

🐾 Tigger and Ollie are both in love with Hermione. And Bea and Jacquelyn both seem to have a crush on Tigger and Ollie.

🐾 Tigger and Ollie act like "the cool kids"; they're "chill." They're also the tallest, so they can reach up and grab branches and reach into trucks to knock over buckets of grain. They can also get really pushy about food and treats, head-butting others! Speaking of head-butting, Bartleby seems to do it for a joke.

🐾 Most of us behave nicely enough, but to be honest, there are three real troublemakers: Bartleby, Dolores, and Violet.

🐾 Our combination of playfulness, agility, and curiosity can lead to some problems. We're famous for nibbling anything, and if we eat the wrong thing, well, there's trouble. Dolores is the worst. She's had three poisoning emergencies! Each time, she's had to eat charcoal to absorb the poison.

But the worst was when she ate a rubber glove. Now, for her own sake, she's in an area where she can't get into as much stuff. Once, a staff member had a pot of chili in the back seat of her truck, and Dolores jumped in and knocked the lid right off. Luckily, she got caught before she could eat more than a bite.

I suppose I'm just tattling. You can't blame me. . . . I've seen everything around here.

"All beings tremble before violence. All fear death. All love life. See yourself in others. Then whom can you hurt? What harm can you do?"
Buddha

Tigger, Hermione, Ollie.

the temperature is below zero. But when we're all together in a herd, we can stay close to one another to make our own heat.

As the humans walk past the stalls, sometimes they stop to sing to the sheep, who love it. Because I'm with four other sheep, I

THE GOAT PEOPLE

In myths, fauns dance and play the flute.

The humans here try to see the world through our eyes. I think of them as the opposite of trolls! In fact, they're a bit like fauns— mythical creatures from ancient Roman mythology.

Fauns were enchanted woodland creatures who had the bodies of humans but the legs, hooves, horns, and tails of goats. Fauns seemed foolish, but they had the special power to help humans.

hear plenty, and I enjoy it, too. "You Are My Sunshine" is everyone's favorite. The camp kids sing to us a lot, and I look forward to hearing your human chorus this week, okay?

Of course, it's not just in the Main

The humans here love to play with us, but they also help people in need, finding new homes for their animals, for example. They also help teach humans about our situation and how it can be avoided.

The humans here have learned exactly how we move around. They also have to climb over our fences!

Barn where rehab happens. Before the big goat rescue happened, Caroline and Nellie were in the Q Field alone. They were older

and hadn't been too active or playful, but when the new goats moved in, they came to life again. If you watch a group of us,

Making friends with both other animals and people (like you!) can heal our broken hearts. Most of us want to become part of a herd.

you'll notice a lot going on. We call to one another, sniff and nuzzle one another, and lie down together (and head-butt, of course).

Because we are herd animals, we stay together, though we are independent individuals for sure. If we lived in the wild, we'd depend upon staying together for safety, more than any other farm animal. There are always bullies in any herd, but we usually only squabble over food, and those fights end pretty fast.

Many of us think of the humans here, at least sometimes, as part of the herd. Some goats, especially Dolores and Violet, love to hang out on the steps of the humans' office building. They can't turn the doorknob, but often the humans let them in for quick visits!

Soon the Q Field contained one big, happy herd. Libby's mom, Leah, nuzzles her all the time!

Lucy the cat lives there, too. Like me, she was once very adventurous. She'd even ride on the back of tractors. Now she's almost twenty, and she stays in the office. The humans really know what makes us

11 NANNY GOATS

The four moms' kids are all grown up now, of course. Forget about the Billy Goats Gruff—the girls all grew into "Nanny Goats Sweet"!

- Edith and Lillian nuzzle and cuddle every night.

- Jacquelyn used to be so shy with people, but she's getting used to them. Jacquelyn's a protective mom; she still follows Lonnie and Loretta everywhere and keeps an eye out for her "adopted" girl, Violet! Jacquelyn's a very attentive mom; she'll call to Loretta from far away to reassure her. But some days, all Jacquelyn wants to do is hang with Tigger and Ollie!

- Vanna's girls, Annie and Tula, totally stick together.

Leah is still called the "best mom." She looks like a zebra, and she's also the biggest paper thief here. Her sweet Libby has a pretty white heart shape on her head.

Loretta standing proud and strong.

miserable and what delights us, and they try to keep us all happy.

What Makes Us Miserable?

- temperatures below zero or above 80 degrees
- lice
- mud
- wet hooves
- sunburn! Some of us white goats burn easily, and the humans use a special livestock sunscreen on us.

What Delights Us?

- adventures with the herd
- hills
- scampering around rocks
- our playground: the seesaw, the swing, the bridge, the barrels, the big wood spool, and the stair structure
- hay piles
- the sound of the food truck coming
- gingersnaps (sheep love these, too)
- big piles of gravel to climb on
- getting into the kitchen (difficult but well worth the effort)
- trucks or tractors parked under leafy trees
- room to roam
- socializing

Seems as if you campers are pretty delighted

with your homemade ice pops. The only creature happier than you guys at the moment seems to be Ollie, who's getting brushed by a volunteer.

Here comes Kathy, the sanctuary's founder, to welcome you to camp. Kathy bought this land and created this place almost twenty years ago. Since then, she and the other humans have rescued more than four thousand animals. And she talks to each one of us every time she comes around.

Awww, did you hear what she just called out to Ollie? She said, "I know . . . it's a beautiful afternoon! I'm so happy for you, Ollie!"

CHAPTER 8

KiDDiNg AROUND

Until about a year ago, I used to play a lot. I had all kinds of naughty adventures, such as the time I got out through the main gate and wandered up the driveway to our neighbor's yard, where I gobbled all the pretty flowers off the shrubs that she took such good care of. This required the humans to create a better gate. Now I keep my adventures in and around the Main Barn.

For most of our lives, many goats are total goofballs. Here, the whole sanctuary is our playground. We're usually jumping and bumping, climbing and scampering, rolling

and pushing against one another, butting and head-wrestling.

Because we are so curious, we put everything in our mouths to check it out, just as human babies do. Most of us love to nibble paper; no one knows why for sure. Maybe it's for the fiber. Violet once ate a ten-dollar bill! We nip at other things, too, such as clothes, mittens, and the corners of long coats. The expression "manners of a goat" means terrible manners—grabby goats! This is true, but I've mellowed in my old age, and the humans now say that I'm rather polite.

We have an actual playground, a lot like the kind you play on. It helps us get our exercise, stay busy, and use up extra energy. (A bored goat is an unhappy goat! Even if we didn't

GOAT JOKES

Jacquelyn's got the "goat giggles"!

We have our own sense of humor, but maybe you'd like to hear some goat jokes that humans seem to find funny.

Why is it hard to carry on a conversation with a goat? Because they're always butting in.

What did the goat say when he woke up on a train? "I have no idea how I goat here."

What do you call a goat's beard? A goatee.

have a playground, we'd still find ways and places to play. There's a tree that's been wrapped in wire mesh so we can't chew the

What did the little goats say when they were caught playing a prank on the sheep? "Sorry, we were just kidding."

How do you keep a goat from charging? You take his credit card away!

Violet's favorite joke is to make driving difficult.

bark, and there's a stick wedged between the tree and the wire. We've been trying to get that stick out for months now.) You just

Violet, Lonnie, and Loretta have always loved the seesaw.

can't stop us. When the vet Dr. Gunzburg kneels down to take care of us, we try to climb right onto his back (and nibble his hair and chomp the papers off his clipboard). "You think I'm a rock, hey, bozos?" he'll say, chuckling. The vets have tough jobs. After all, we can never tell them what's wrong. We speak a different language!

We love playing King of the Castle
(in Loretta's case, Princess of the Hay Pile).

OUR PLAYGROUND!

We also love barrels to roll and butt with our heads, large tractor tires, plastic igloos or houses to climb on, tree stumps of different heights to jump on like stepping stones, or wagons or trailers to jump into (or eat hay from!).

Annie, Libby, and Iris kidding around. When we get really excited during play, we make a funny noise that sounds like a combination of a sneeze and a fart!

We love our bridges, no matter how low.

The Swing Table!

The Jungle Gym!

STENCiL:
THE PERFECT PLAYMATE

I can't talk about play without telling you about Stencil, the gentle, silky-eared Nubian goat.

Stencil was named for his unusual pattern, which looked like a map of the United States!

It's too bad he died. He would've loved playing with you this week.

He was rescued in 2010 with eighteen others. All the goats were too thin. But Stencil loved his food, and he was an expert snack stealer. Once, he waited near a visitor's car as she parked. As she opened her car door to get out, there was two-hundred-pound Stencil with his hooves on her legs, snarfing down her sandwich so fast she hardly knew it was happening!

Stencil was famous for following camp kids around. As soon as they arrived in the morning, he'd run toward them, his ears flopping, and he'd stay close to them all day (except at feeding time)!

Stencil was a genius at giving and receiving love. We all miss him so much. It's a lucky thing that goats and humans have such good memories.

Kids just naturally put their hands on Stencil's back as they walked together.

CHAPTER 9

GOATS IN COATS

The herd's health continued to improve through their first full winter. But winter weather was tough on all of us, as usual. The humans go into "winter mode," listing warnings for the staff, like these on the big whiteboard:

* When walking horses, watch the roads for ice and don't walk where the roads get steep.

* All hoses must be drained and disconnected or they will freeze. The big pig hose was frozen into the ground this week!

* If it's below freezing, put coats on Caroline, Lucia, and Ollie.

Caroline gets an extra-special goat coat.

Some winter days are warm enough to go without my coat.

It gets so cold, you can even see rooster breath!

When it's really, really cold, the birds in unheated spaces are brought into the office to spend the night in wire cages. We get nice warm drinking water, and the humans check to make sure that our extra straw bedding is dry and there are no drafts. Some stalls are heated with overhead heaters. We seniors get extra food. Our bodies are working so hard to keep warm that we need the extra calories. (Weight gain = wider bellies!) As we eat, you can see our breath in the frosty air.

One early morning during a snowstorm, a volunteer walked by my stall. She'd driven to the sanctuary on bad roads to help out, and

she'd slipped on the ice on the road into the barn, where she'd come to prepare our food. "I wish all I had to do is curl up in a warm stall and watch winter happen!" she said, laughing with another volunteer. In that storm, the humans had to worry about the hay delivery and then pay extra for it—but they always, always find a way. We never have to think about it.

How to Keep Warm in Winter

- Curl up with a buddy.
- Enjoy your new layer of straw bedding.
- Eat more hay. The slow digestion process makes our insides warm.
- If you have a nice layer of fat and a good undercoat, appreciate it!
- Wear your goat coat.

Winter always passes, and soon enough, our coats go back into storage. When spring comes, the humans do all the change-of-season chores. They have to check all the sanctuary fences and gates for winter damage, and they clean and disinfect all the animals' housing. It's a lot of work.

MORE THAN COATS

Atlas quickly learned how to use his wheels. Soon he moved as well as any other goat!

In addition to giving us coats, humans have figured out lots of ways to keep us comfortable and healthy.

For instance, my old friend Atlas arrived with deformed legs because of bad hooves. His knees were swollen to the size of oranges, and he could barely move. But the humans created a goat wheelchair for him!

The humans are so happy when winter turns to spring!

As spring turns to summer, ferns sprout and bloom. Soon it's so hot and humid that the humans have to carry their water bottles all the time. The Main Barn doors stays open for whatever breeze might come through, and when we're out of the barn, we look for shade. And another bunch of camp kids arrive.

When autumn comes, almost every leaf on every tree changes color. Some are the color of fire.

Green springs turn into even greener summers.

Almost a year since the herd arrived, every rescued goat roamed free.

PART 4

RELEASE

Roaming Free

CHAPTER 10

THE UNDERFOOT FAMILY

The entire point of the first three *R*'s—rescue, recovery, and rehabilitation—is to get to the fourth *R*, which is the best of all. It's the prize at the end ... better than a gingersnap before sundown. The fourth *R* is release!

Other animals at different kinds of sanctuaries may be released back into the wild, but the animals here don't come from the wild in the first place. Our breeds have

been kept by humans on farms for so long, there's no wilderness where we belong. So we stay here. For us, "release" means being able to leave our stalls during the day to spend time with our herd and walk free. For many of us, that means joining the famous Underfoot Family. Once the humans decide that we're ready to wander, the change is simple and fast. They just open our stall doors, stand back, and watch.

Each of us handles that moment differently. For instance, Hermione took a few steps out of her stall, stayed frozen there a long time, took a few careful steps forward, then froze for another long moment before taking a few more steps. Some just stand at the entrance, not knowing what to do, then turn around and go back into their stalls for the rest of the day. The goofier and more confident goats run right out and start jumping and playing, as if to say, *Hey, I'm free! Let me go have some fun! Let me go cause trouble!* Some look to other Underfoot Family members for reassurance; those members approach the "new kids" to show them that they're invited and accepted into the family. Eventually we all feel a good vibe from the happy Underfoot animals around us; that lets us know we're all set.

Imagine that you had recess all day, and you and your friends could just wander around your school and its neighborhood, making all your own decisions and playing and getting into mischief as much as you wanted. That's what it's like to be a member of the Underfoot Family. We are let out in the morning, we wander freely all day, and then we're led back to our stalls to sleep.

In the Underfoot Family, different species make friends.

Usually, we goats hang with the sheep. Sometimes all the senior folks will stay together and let the younger creatures be wild. Often, the three Nubians (Ollie, Tigger, and Hermione) stick together. And, of course, the Q goats are their own roaming family within their own field.

Being a member of the Underfoot Family has a major benefit: when the hay truck leaves messes of extra hay along its way, we can be right there to help clean up the leftovers. I used to love my early-morning surprise breakfast buffet. We can also scoot under the horse fence just a little bit to steal some of the horses' food. Shhh!

And it's not only goats and sheep who are part of the Underfoot Family!

Karma the duck doesn't let arthritis stop her.

Al the rooster's excited about spring ... and lunch!

Gilbert the goose after a spring rain.

CHAPTER 11

ONE GRATEFUL GOAT

Wow, is your first day over already? I seem to have told you everything in one day. Tomorrow, I suppose, another animal will greet you and do the same.

Anyway, kids, I loved following you around. I hope you enjoy the rest of your week and that you'll keep listening, like you did today.

We have so much to tell you.

LADY LUCIA'S LIFE LESSONS

Before you go home, I'd like to share just a little more wisdom. Here's what I've learned about being a goat and having a happy life, and I think it may work for you, too.

- Enjoy your own weirdness—no apologies!
- Stand your ground with confidence. Stay sturdy on your feet.
- Take time to play—"enjoy the goof"!
- Climb to the top of your own hill and look around. Enjoy the view.
- It's okay to disagree (butt heads!) once in a while . . . friends and family can always make up.

Climb to the top!

A LETTER FROM THE AUTHOR:
A WORLD AWAY

When I was a kid, I loved feeding the goats and sheep at petting zoos. My dad would give me a dime to put into what looked like a gumball machine, and a handful of dusty grain pellets would pour into my palm. I couldn't wait to feel the animals' fuzzy lips on my hand, and I felt very popular as they crowded around, pushing one another out of the way to get to the treats!

Catskill Animal Sanctuary is a two-hour drive from my New York City apartment, but it's a world away. When I first visited, it became clear that it was no petting zoo. As a matter of fact, in researching goats before my visit, I learned that petting zoos usually aren't good places for animals. All those grain pellets aren't healthy for the animals, and the animals don't really live there—they have to get on trucks and leave every day, which is very stressful for them.

Most of the time, animals don't like crowds of strangers running up to touch them, and the humans in charge of those petting zoos usually don't teach people how to behave around animals.

At the sanctuary, visitors are carefully taught to move slowly and speak softly, at least at first. Only the animals that like to be touched are to be petted. And nobody has to pay when they enter—it's not a zoo.

It was 12 degrees the day of my first visit, and even the air looked frosty. I sat bundled up on the floor in Lucia's stall. I watched her and the four sheep quietly munch their afternoon hay. (I even tasted a little—it was very dry. If I had to eat more, I would at least insist on some salad dressing!)

Lucia stood nicely, like a small white camel. Right away I knew that this gentle lady should be the narrator of this book. When I told that to Kathy, she clapped her hands, and said, "Oh, that's great! She's got so much to say!" Kellie, the staff member who had bottle-fed baby Violet, agreed. "The only thing is," she said, "she's probably at the end of her life right now. Will that be a problem?"

"Not at all," I said. "She's alive now, so I can still get to know her."

Lucia had been having a hard time moving around, and just a few months after I visited, her legs gave out and she had a bad fall. A health-care assistant, Laura, curled up on the floor next to her overnight to keep an eye on her. Lucia stood right over her, resting her nose on Laura's forehead all night long.

A few days later, I was at my desk, writing this book, when I got an email from sanctuary staffers Veronica Finnegan and Kelly Mullins. "I have some sad news," it began. Of course, I knew what that news was. I sighed and kept reading:

"Our beautiful Lucia passed away on Saturday afternoon surrounded by her loving and heartbroken caregivers. She left us peacefully, with the assitance of our wonderful vet Dr. Mark Rosenberg.

"Eighteen is very old for a goat. Her body had been failing little by little and she was often unable to getup without assitance. During the brutal cold snap, she was brought into the infirmary to sleep in a heated stall.

"But the time had finally come on Saturday, when her quality of life had gotten so poor that we had to make the most loving choice we could, for her sake."

I was both sad and happy to read this. Sad that this sweet lady was gone from our lives, but happy that I got to meet her and help tell her story . . . and the story of the sanctuary and all the creatures who call it home.

— Kama Aichann

Me at the petting zoo not far from the sanctuary.

Lucia
2000–2018

GLOSSARY

adapt: adjust or get used to

agile: able to move quickly and easily

anemia: a health condition in which a mammal doesn't have enough healthy red blood cells to supply his or her tissues with oxygen, making him or her feel tired and weak

chamber: a closed-in space, a compartment

colostrum: thick yellow milk that a doe feeds her newborn kid. Colostrum is high in protein, vitamins, and antibodies to protect kids from infection.

cud: partly digested food returned to the mouth from the first stomach of ruminants for further chewing

deformed: not formed or developed normally

domesticated: brought up among humans. A domesticated animal needs to be cared for by humans. Dogs and cats are domesticated; so are most farm animals in the United States.

fiber: coarse plant matter found in fruits, vegetables, grains, legumes

girth: the measurement around the middle of something, such as a person's waist

graze: to feed on land covered by grass

herbivore: an animal that eats only plants

herd: a group of goats. Herds can have as many as forty goats.

maternal: motherly

neglect: to ignore or care for improperly or even cruelly

neuter: to operate on males to keep them from fathering babies

prehensile: having the ability to grasp

ruminant: an animal with a four-chambered stomach who chews his or her cud

thrive: develop well, prosper, flourish

HOW YOU CAN HELP

🐾 Learn more at casanctuary.org. Visit the sanctuary (or any animal sanctuary in your area) and meet the animals yourself! Tell others what you learned there.

🐾 Consider becoming a vegan or eating less meat, dairy, and eggs, if you eat animal products now.

🐾 Donate to the sanctuary. It costs a lot each year to feed and house just one goat. Try a bake sale selling Lucia's favorite gingersnaps! (see page 138 for recipe).

CAMP KINDNESS KIDS' FAVORITE RECIPES

Vegans do not eat meat, eggs, or dairy (milk, ice cream, cheese, yogurt).

GOOD 'N' GOATY GINGERSNAPS (FOR PEOPLE!)

Goats love their gingersnap treats . . . and so do people.

- 1 ¼ cups sugar
- ¾ cup vegan butter sticks, softened
- ⅓ cup molasses
- 3 tablespoons soy or almond milk

- 1 teaspoon vanilla
- 2 ¼ cups flour
- 2 teaspoons baking soda
- 1 teaspoon ground cinnamon
- 1 teaspoon ground ginger

1. Preheat oven to 350°F. Line a baking tray with parchment paper.

2. In a bowl, beat 1 cup of the sugar and the vegan butter until creamy. Stir in the molasses, soy or almond milk, and vanilla.

3. Add flour, baking soda, cinnamon, and ginger and mix well.

4. Place the remaining ¼ cup of sugar in a shallow dish. Shape dough into walnut-size balls and roll them in the sugar.

5. Place rolled dough in rows 2 inches apart on the baking tray.

6. Bake 9 to 11 minutes or until bottoms are lightly browned. Transfer to a plate or wire rack to cool. Makes about 2 dozen cookies.

TEMPEH TACOS

You don't need meat to make tacos! Like tofu, tempeh is made from soybeans and is a great source of protein. You can find it near the tofu in many grocery stores.

- 1 (8-ounce) package tempeh
- 1 cup diced tomatoes (canned or fresh)
- ½ cup soy or tamari sauce
- ½ onion, diced
- ½ green bell pepper, diced
- 2 cloves garlic, minced
- 2 teaspoons chili powder
- 2 teaspoons garlic powder
- 2 teaspoons dried oregano
- 2 teaspoons lime juice
- 1 teaspoon cumin

- 2 tablespoons olive oil
- 2 tablespoons water
- 1 package of taco shells or soft corn tortillas. For serving (choose whatever you like!)
- guacamole or diced avocado
- salsa
- vegan cheddar cheese
- vegan sour cream
- black olives
- cilantro

1. Grate or mince the tempeh.

2. In a bowl, mix the tempeh, tomatoes, tamari or soy, onion, bell pepper, garlic, chili powder, garlic powder, oregano, lime juice, and cumin.

3. Heat a pan over medium heat, then add the oil. Once the oil is hot, add the tempeh mixture and water.

4. Cook, stirring occasionally, for about 10 minutes, or until the onions and bell peppers are soft and the tempeh has browned.

5. Fill shells with the tempeh mixture and choose your toppings! Serves 6 to 8.

BERRY DELICIOUS SMOOTHIE BOWL

Smoothie bowls are like smoothies, but much thicker! They're like ice-cream sundaes with lots of delicious toppings. You can change most of the ingredients depending on what you like, but always use a banana to create a thick, creamy base.

- 1 cup chopped kale or baby spinach
- 1 cup frozen blueberries
- 1 cup frozen strawberries

- 1 frozen banana (If your bananas aren't frozen, add 3 or 4 ice cubes when blending.)
- up to 1 cup unsweetened nondairy milk (soy, almond, coconut, rice, oat, or hemp)

Suggested Toppings:

- sliced bananas
- sliced strawberries
- fresh blueberries
- dried fruit
- granola

- hemp seeds
- sunflower seeds
- toasted or raw coconut
- mini vegan chocolate chips

Puree all ingredients in a blender until smooth. Pour your smoothie into a bowl, then add whatever toppings you like. Makes two bowls.

Thanks to the vegan chefs Linda Soper-Kolton and Sara Boan of Compassionate Cuisine (casanctuary.org/compassionate-cuisine).

PHOTO CREDITS

All photos by Janet Holmes
(frogoutofwater.com) except:

52 (map): Tara Wright

74 (goat stomachs): Tara Wright

79: Shutterstock/ Eivor Kuchta

84, 89, 116, 142: Miles O'Reilly

93, 113: Erica Ritter

94: Shutterstock/Danilo Sanino

97: Christiane Bailey

ACKNOWLEDGMENTS

Michelle Alvarez

Lauren Barbieri

Becca Bazell

Sara Boan

Veronica Finnegan

Dr. David Gunzburg
and Hurley Veterinary
Hospital

Jamey Hecht

Janet Holmes

Anne Hulett

Lesley Johnson

Kaden Maguire

Kelly Mullins

Kellie Myers

Miles O'Reilly

Alicia Pell, Harry Lynch,
and Tracey Stewart of
Farm Sanctuary

Erica Ritter

Linda Soper-Kolton

Erica Zappy Wainer

INDEX

photo credit: Nicholas Noyes

Kama Einhorn is a humane educator, animal welfare advocate, and author of more than forty books for children and teachers. Animals are her people. She lives in Brooklyn, New York.

Janet Holmes has always loved animals. As she spent time experiencing animals as individuals through the lens of her camera, she committed to donating her photography services to animal rescue groups . . . and to give at least half of her profits to support animal rescue. You can see more of her photos at www.frogoutofwater.ca.

photo credit: Miles O'Reilly